Easy Learning C#

YANG HU

Simple is the beginning of wisdom. From the essence of practice, this book to briefly explain the concept and vividly cultivate programming interest, you will learn it easy and fast.

http://en.verejava.com

Copyright © 2019 Yang Hu
All rights reserved.
ISBN: 9781092788007

CONTENTS

1. Visual Studio Express for Windows installation 3
2. C# basic concept 7
   2.1 C# HelloWorld 7
   2.2 Variable 8
   2.3 Base Data Type 9
   2.4 Constant 11
   2.5 Data Type Conversion 12
3. C# Operator 13
   3.1 Arithmetic Operator 13
   3.2 Relational Operator 15
   3.3 Logical Operator 16
4. C# Control Statement 18
   4.1 If Conditional Statement 18
   4.2 Switch Branch Statement 19
   4.3 While Loop 21
   4.4 While Loop Games 23
   4.5 For Loop 25
   4.6 For Loop Bubble Ball Example 27
5. Array 28
   5.1 One-Dimensional Array 28
   5.2 Two-Dimensional Array 30
   5.3 Two-Dimensional Array Minesweeper 32
6. Struct 34
7. C# Object Oriented 35
   7.1 Class 35
   7.2 Encapsulation Method 36
   7.3 Constructor Method 38
   7.4 Method Overload 40
   7.5 Static Keyword 41
   7.6 Inheritance 43
   7.7 Method Override 45
   7.8 Abstract Class 47

- 7.9 Interface 49
- 7.10 Enum 51
- 7.11 Polymorphism 54
- 8. Thread 59
- 9. Exception 61
- 10. String 63
  - 10.1 String Functions 63
  - 10.2 String and StringBuilder 67
- 11. Date 68
- 12. Collection Data Structure 70
  - 12.1 Generic 70
  - 12.2 List 71
  - 12.3 Queue 73
  - 12.4 Stack 75
  - 12.5 Hashtable 77
- 13. File and Directory 79
  - 13.1 File 79
  - 13.2 Directory 81

Visual Studio Express for Windows installation

Download
en_visual_studio_express_2015_for_windows_desktop_x86_x64_web_installer_6846484.zip

https://visualstudio.microsoft.com/downloads/
or
http://en.verejava.com/download.jsp?id=1

Upzip and then Setup Visual Studio Express 2015 for Windows always click next

Open Visual Studio Express 2015

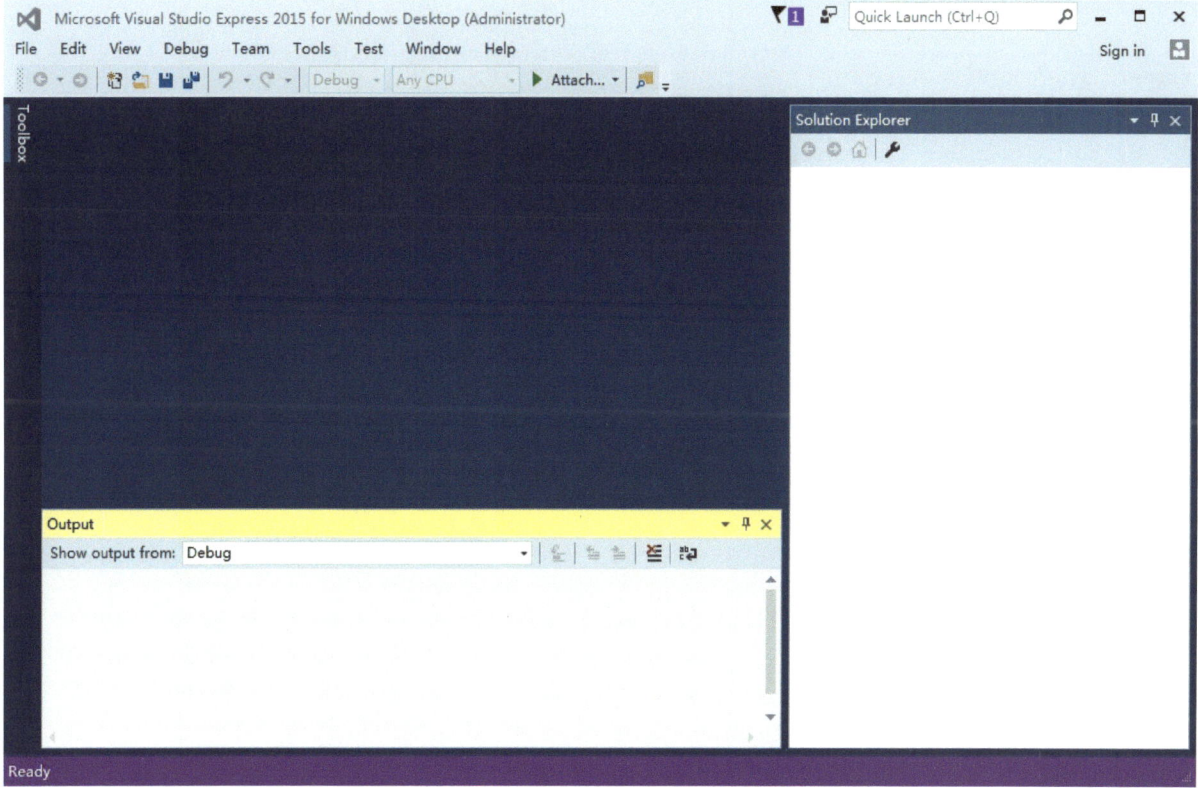

Click on File -> New Project ... to create a new C# Console Application

Visual C# -> Console Application

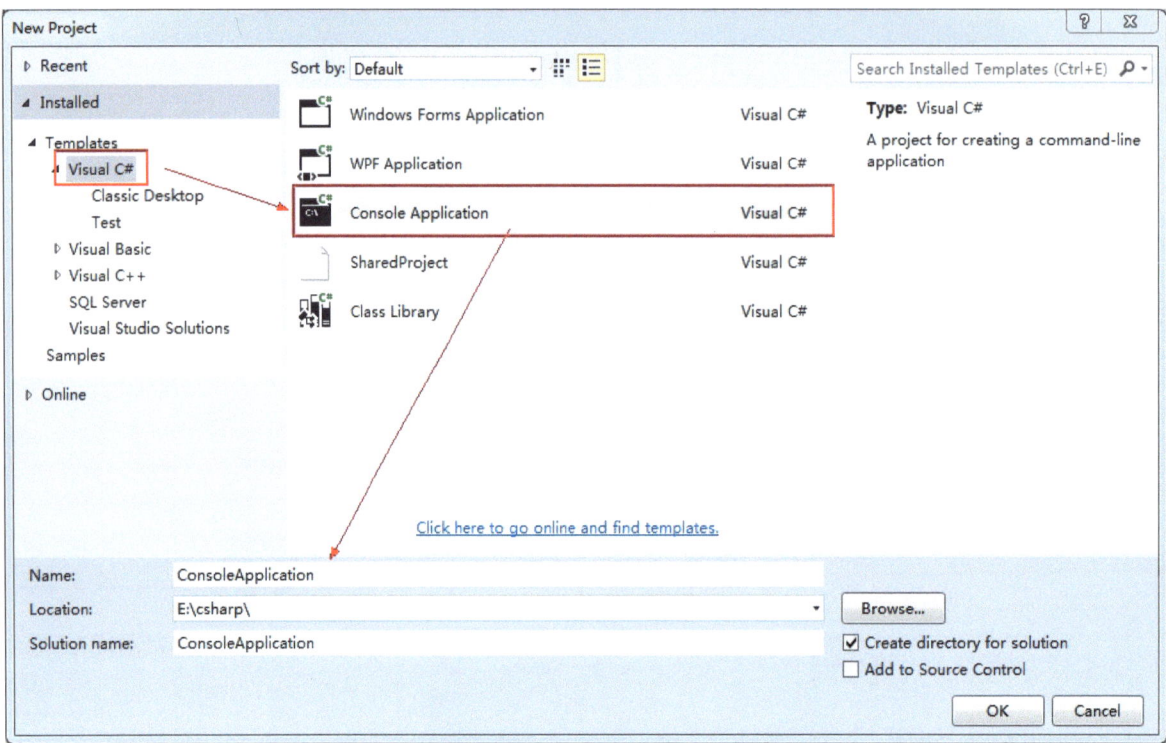

Click on the Program.cs under Solution Explorer.

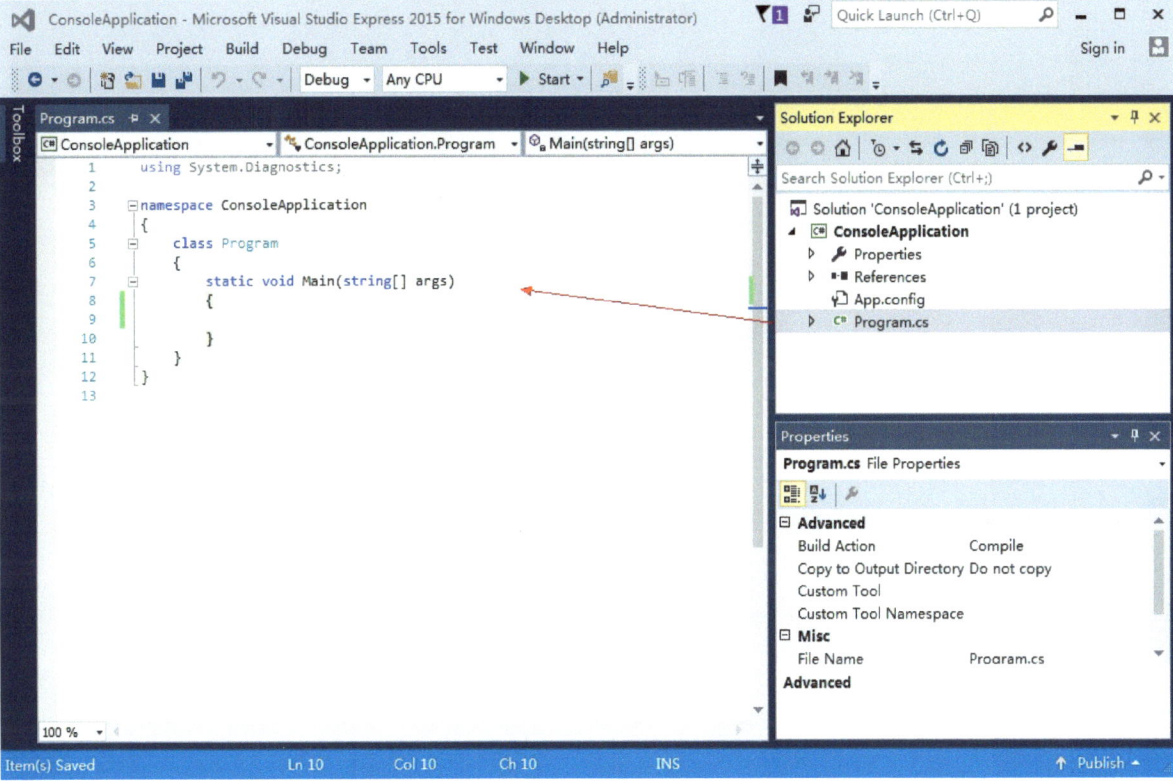

Enter the code : Debug.WriteLine("Hello World"); Then click the start button to run the program and you will see the Output window: Hello World

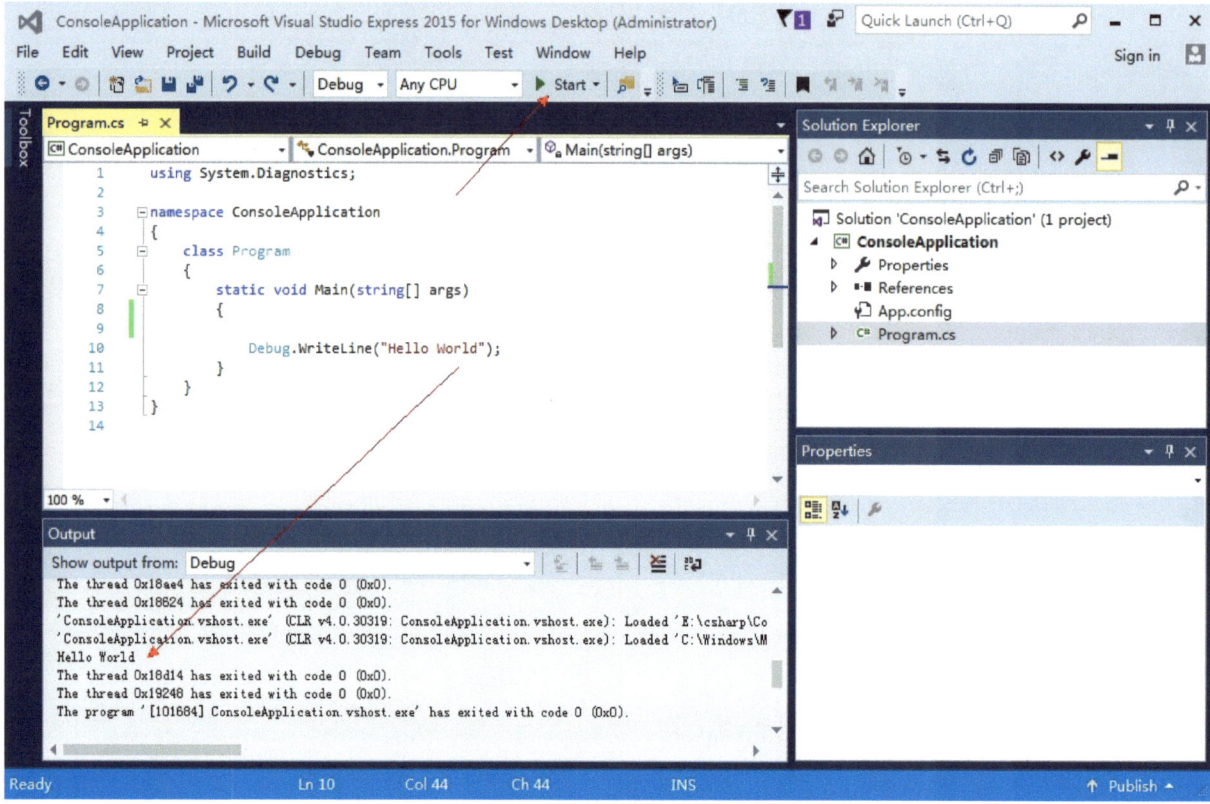

C# HelloWorld

//: is comment can not be executed
namespace: is a folder
Main: is the entry to the program execution.

1. Create file: HelloWorld.cs

```csharp
using System.Diagnostics; // import system namespace

namespace ConsoleApplication
{
    class HelloWorld
    {
        static void Main(string[] args)
        {
            //Print the Hello Word to the console and then \n wrap a new line
            Debug.WriteLine("Hello Word\n");
            Debug.WriteLine("Good start is half the success");
        }
    }
}
```

Result:

Hello Word
Good start is half the success

Variable

Variable: a memory area allocated by the system to store data
string: Character enclosed in double quotes " ". like "Apple", "Orange"

1. Create file: TestVariable.cs

```csharp
using System.Diagnostics;

namespace ConsoleApplication
{
    class TestVariable
    {
        static void Main(string[] args)
        {
            //string "mineral water" is stored in the variable of cup.
            string cup = "mineral water";

            //Print the data of cup
            Debug.WriteLine(cup);

            //Replace the value of the cup by "Coke"
            cup = "Coke";
            Debug.WriteLine(cup);

            //Delete the variable
            cup = null;
            Debug.WriteLine(cup);
        }
    }
}
```

Result:

mineral water
Coke

Base Data Type

C# Base Data Type
    1. Integer(byte,short,int,long)
    2. Floating (float,double)
    3. Character(char)
    4. Boolean (bool)

Create file: BaseDataType.cs

1. byte,short,int,long

```csharp
using System.Diagnostics;
namespace ConsoleApplication
{
    class BaseDataType
    {
        static void Main(string[] args)
        {
            //Integer(byte,short,int,long)
            byte a1 = 1;       //byte = 8 bits -2^7~2^7-1(-128~127)
            short a2 = 10;     //short 2 bytes = 16 bits -2^15~2^15-1
            int a3 = 100;      //int 4 bytes = 32 bits -2^31~2^31-1
            long a4 = 1000;    //long 8 bytes = 64 bits -2^63~2^63-1
            Debug.WriteLine(a1);
            Debug.WriteLine(a2);
            Debug.WriteLine(a3);
            Debug.WriteLine(a4);
        }
    }
}
```

Result:

1
10
100
1000

2. float,double,char,bool

```csharp
using System.Diagnostics;
namespace ConsoleApplication
{
    class BaseDataType
    {
        static void Main(string[] args)
        {
            //Floating point(float,double)
            double b1 = 10.1;   //double 8 bytes = 64 bits
            float b2 = 12.2f;   //float 4 bytes = 32 bits
            Debug.WriteLine(b1);
            Debug.WriteLine(b2);

            //char is a single character enclosed in single quotes' '
            char c1 = 'a';    // char 2 bytes = 16 bits
            Debug.WriteLine(c1);

            bool d1 = true;  //boolean 1 byte = 8 bits
            bool d2 = false;
            Debug.WriteLine(d1);
            Debug.WriteLine(d2);
        }
    }
}
```

Result:

10.1
12.2
a
True
False

Constant

Constant: the value can not be changed

1. Create file: FinalVariable.cs

```csharp
using System.Diagnostics;
namespace ConsoleApplication
{
    class FinalVariable
    {
        static void Main(string[] args)
        {
            //1. Integer constant
            const int UP = 0;
            const int DOWN = 1;
            Debug.WriteLine(UP);
            Debug.WriteLine(DOWN);

            //2. Floating constants
            const float PI = 3.14f;
            Debug.WriteLine(PI);

            //3. Boolean constants
            const bool RUN = true;
            Debug.WriteLine(RUN);

            //4. Character constants
            const char A = 'A';
        }
    }
}
```

Result:
0
1
3.14
True
A

Data Type Conversion

1. Create file: TypeConvert.cs

```csharp
using System.Diagnostics;
namespace ConsoleApplication
{
    class TypeConvert
    {
        static void Main(string[] args)
        {
            byte varByte = 1;
            int varInt = 2;
            //Small integer directly converted to a large integer
            varInt = varByte;
            Debug.WriteLine(varInt);

            byte varBtye2 = 1;
            int varInt2 = 2;
            //Large integer are converted to small integer require a cast.
            varBtye2 = (byte)varInt2;
            Debug.WriteLine(varBtye2);

            //string connection +
            string str = "one door close, " + " anther door will open";
            Debug.WriteLine(str2);
        }
    }
}
```

Result:

1
2
one door close, anther door will open

Arithmetic Operator

Arithmetic operation:
   add +, minus -, multiply *, divisible /, take modulo %, decrement ---, increase ++

Create file: ArithmeticOperator.cs

1. add +, minus -, multiply *, divisible /, take modulo %

```csharp
using System.Diagnostics;
namespace ConsoleApplication
{
    class ArithmeticOperator
    {
        static void Main(string[] args)
        {
            int a = 1;
            int b = 2;
            int c = 3;
            Debug.WriteLine(a + b);
            Debug.WriteLine(a - b);
            Debug.WriteLine(a * b);
            Debug.WriteLine(a / b);
            Debug.WriteLine(c % b); // remaining number after the division
        }
    }
}
```

Result:

```
3
-1
2
0
1
```

2. decrement ---, increase ++

```
using System.Diagnostics;
namespace ConsoleApplication
{
    class ArithmeticOperator
    {
        static void Main(string[] args)
        {
            int d = 4;
            Debug.WriteLine(d++); // ++ after the d output and then increment by 1

            d = 4;
            Debug.WriteLine(++d); // ++ after d increment by 1 and then output

            d = 4;
            Debug.WriteLine(d--); // -- after the d output and then decremented by 1

            d = 4;
            Debug.WriteLine(--d); // -- after d decremented by 1 and then output
        }
    }
}
```

Result:

4
5
4
3

Relational Operator

Relational operator: only two results: true or false

1. Create file: RelationalOperator.cs

```csharp
using System.Diagnostics;

namespace ConsoleApplication
{
    class RelationalOperator
    {
        static void Main(string[] args)
        {
            Debug.WriteLine(100 > 200);
            Debug.WriteLine(100 >= 100);
            Debug.WriteLine(100 < 200);
            Debug.WriteLine(100 <= 200);
            Debug.WriteLine(100 == 100);
            Debug.WriteLine(100 != 200);
        }
    }
}
```

Result:

false
true
true
true
true
true

Logical Operator

Logical Operator: and &&, or ||, not !
    1. && returns true if both sides of the operation are true, otherwise false
    2. || The result is false when both sides of the operation are false, otherwise true;
    3. ! if returns true, the result is false, otherwise is true

1. Create file: LogicalOperator.cs

```
using System.Diagnostics;
namespace ConsoleApplication
{
    class LogicalOperator
    {
        static void Main(string[] args)
        {
            Debug.WriteLine(true && false);
            Debug.WriteLine(false && true);
            Debug.WriteLine(false && false);
            Debug.WriteLine(true && true);

            Debug.WriteLine(true || false);
            Debug.WriteLine(false || true);
            Debug.WriteLine(true || true);
            Debug.WriteLine(false || false);

            Debug.WriteLine(!true);
            Debug.WriteLine(!false);
        }
    }
}
```

Result:
false
false
false
true
----
true
true
true
false
----
false
true

2. && and ||

```csharp
using System.Diagnostics;
namespace ConsoleApplication
{
    class LogicalOperator
    {
        static void Main(string[] args)
        {

            bool b = true;
            Debug.WriteLine(b);
            Debug.WriteLine(1 > 2 && b);
            Debug.WriteLine(2 > 1 && b);

            Debug.WriteLine("--------------");
            bool b1 = true;
            Debug.WriteLine(b1);
            Debug.WriteLine(2 > 1 || b1);
            Debug.WriteLine(1 > 2 || b1);
        }
    }
}
```

Result:

true
false
true
----
true
true
true

If Conditional Statement

If statement
1. if(expression){statement}
2. if (expression) { statement } else { statement }
3. if (expression) {statement} else if { statement }

Payroll tax example:
Tax amount = (basic salary -3500) * tax rate
level:
500 -- 2000 $: 10% tax rate
2000--20000 $:   tax rate 20%
More than 20000$:   tax rate 30%

```csharp
using System.Diagnostics;
namespace ConsoleApplication
{
  class IfStatement
  {
    static void Main(string[] args)
    {
      int salary = 23500;// basic salary
      int extra = salary - 3500;// excess tax is required
      double tax = 0; //tax amount
      if (extra >= 500 && extra < 2000)
      {
        tax = extra * 0.1;
      }
      else if (extra >= 2000 && extra < 20000)
      {
        tax = extra * 0.2;
      }
      else
      {
        tax = extra * 0.3;
      }
      Debug.WriteLine("tax amount=" + tax);
    }
  }
}
```

Result:
tax amount=6000

Switch Branch Statement

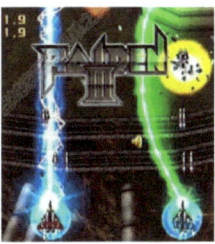

Keyboard input a number 0, 1 , 2, 3
0 : The airplane moves up
1 : The airplane moves down
2 : The airplane moves to the left
3: The airplane moves to the right
Otherwise the airplane does not move

```csharp
class SwitchStatement
{
    static void Main(string[] args)
    {
        Debug.WriteLine("Keyboard enters a number 0: up, 1: down, 2: left, 3: right");
        int num = Convert.ToInt32(Console.ReadLine());
        switch (num)
        {
            case 0:
                Debug.WriteLine("Airplane moves up");
                break; //terminate the code to execute
            case 1:
                Debug.WriteLine("Airplane moves down");
                break;
            case 2:
                Debug.WriteLine("Airplane moves to the left");
                break;
            case 3:
                Debug.WriteLine("Airplane moves to the right");
                break;
            default:
                Debug.WriteLine("Airplane does not move");
                break;
        }
    }
}
```

Result:
Keyboard enters a number 0: up, 1: down, 2: left, 3: right
1
Airplane moves down

Run again:
Keyboard enters a number 0: up, 1: down, 2: left, 3: right
2
Airplane moves to the left

While Loop

```
int i = 0;
while (i < 10)          i=0 < 10 true executes the loop code
{
   Debug.WriteLine(i + "\n");
   i++;                 i=1
}


while (i < 10)          i=1 < 10 true executes the loop code
{
   Debug.WriteLine(i + "\n");
   i++;                 i=2
}


while (i < 10)          i=2 < 10 true executes the loop code
{
   Debug.WriteLine(i + "\n");
   i++;                 i=3
}
           Until i = 9

while (i < 10)          i=9 < 10 true executes the loop code
{
   Debug.WriteLine(i + "\n");
   i++;                 i=10
}


   while (i < 10)       i=10 < 10 False terminated
   {
      Debug.WriteLine(i + "\n");
      i++;              i=11
   }
```

* While Loop is terminated

while loop

while(expression){

}
if the expression is continues execute 1, otherwise exits the loop

```csharp
using System.Diagnostics;
using System;
namespace ConsoleApplication
{
    class WhileLoop
    {
        static void Main(string[] args)
        {
            int i = 0;
            while (i < 10) //if (i<10) true executes the loop, otherwise is terminated
            {
                Debug.WriteLine(i);
                i++;
            }
        }
    }
}
```

Result:

0
1
2
3
4
5
6
7
8
9

While Loop Games

While (num!= 0){
    if num equal 1: watermelon
    else if num equal 2: banana
    else if num equal 3: peach
    else if num equal 0: thunder
}

```csharp
class WhileLoopGame
{
    static void Main(string[] args)
    {
        Debug.WriteLine("Keyboard Input 1: Watermelon, 2: Banana, 3: Peach, 0: Thunder ");
        int num = 0;
        while (num != -1) //If you enter -1 to terminate the game
        {
            num = Convert.ToInt32(Console.ReadLine());
            if (num == 1)
            {
                Debug.WriteLine("You cut the watermelon");
            }
            else if (num == 2)
            {
                Debug.WriteLine("You cut the banana");
            }
            else if (num == 3)
            {
                Debug.WriteLine("You cut the peach");
            }
            else if (num == 0)
            {
                Debug.WriteLine("You cut the thunder, game to terminate");
            }
        }
    }
}
```

Result:

```
Keyboard Input 1: Watermelon, 2: Banana, 3: Peach, 0: Thunder
1
You cut the watermelon
2
You cut the banana
3
You cut the peach
0
You cut the thunder game termination
```

For Loop

for (initialization variable; condition; update variable){
    statement;
}

```
for (int i = 0; i < 10; i++)     i=0 < 10 true executes the loop code
{
   Debug.Write(i + " , ");       i++
}

for (int i = 0; i < 10; i++)     i=1 < 10 true executes the loop code
{
   Debug.Write(i + " , ");       i++
}

for (int i = 0; i < 10; i++)     i=2 < 10 true executes the loop code
{
   Debug.Write(i + " , ");       i++
}
                 Until i = 9
for (int i = 0; i < 10; i++)     i=9 < 10 true executes the loop code
{
   Debug.Write(i + " , ");       i++
}

for (int i = 0; i < 10; i++)     i=10 < 10 False terminated
{
   Debug.Write(i + " , ");       i++
}

        For Loop is terminated
```

1. Create file: ForLoop.cs

```csharp
using System.Diagnostics;

namespace ConsoleApplication
{
    class ForLoop
    {
        static void Main(string[] args)
        {
            for (int i = 0; i < 10; i++)
            {
                Debug.Write(i + " , ");
            }
        }
    }
}
```

Result:

0 , 1 , 2 , 3 , 4 , 5 , 6 , 7 , 8 , 9 ,

For Loop Bubble Ball Example

Bubble ball game:
 the game starts with 64 balls,
    requiring 8 balls per line. * is ball

1. Create file: ForLoop.cs

```csharp
using System.Diagnostics;
namespace ConsoleApplication
{
    class ForStatement2
    {
        static void Main(string[] args)
        {
            for (int i = 1; i <= 64; i++)
            {
                Debug.Write("* ");
                if (i % 8 == 0) // 8%8==0 , 16%8==0 , 24 %8==0, 32%8==0 , 48%8==0 , 64%8==0
                {
                    Debug.WriteLine("");// Wrap one line
                }
            }
        }
    }
}
```

Result:
* * * * * * * *
* * * * * * * *
* * * * * * * *
* * * * * * * *
* * * * * * * *
* * * * * * * *
* * * * * * * *
* * * * * * * *

One-Dimensional Array

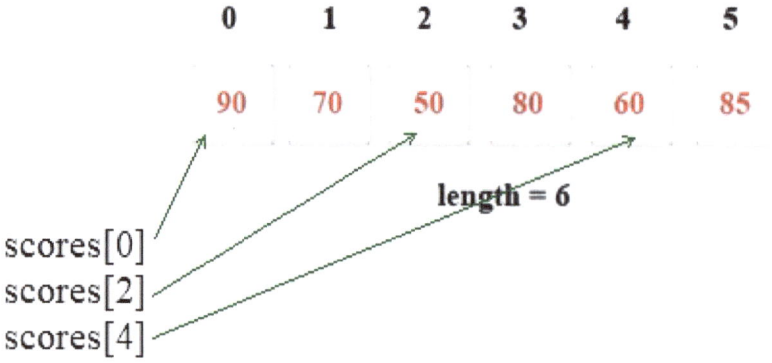

1. Create file: OneArray.cs

```
using System.Diagnostics;

namespace ConsoleApplication
{
    class OneArray
    {
        static void Main(string[] args)
        {
            // Statically define a one-dimensional array
            int[] scores = { 90, 70, 50, 80, 60, 85 };

            Debug.WriteLine(scores[0]);
            Debug.WriteLine(scores[2]);
            Debug.WriteLine(scores[4]);
        }
    }
}
```

Result:

```
90
50
60
```

2. Print all the data of the scores:

```csharp
using System.Diagnostics;

namespace ConsoleApplication
{
    class OneArray
    {
        static void Main(string[] args)
        {
            int[] scores = { 90, 70, 50, 80, 60, 85 };

            //One-dimensional array traversal, print the score of the array
            for (int i = 0; i < scores.Length; i++)
            {
                Debug.Write(scores[i] + ",");
            }
        }
    }
}
```

Result:

90,70,50,80,60,85,

Two-Dimensional Array

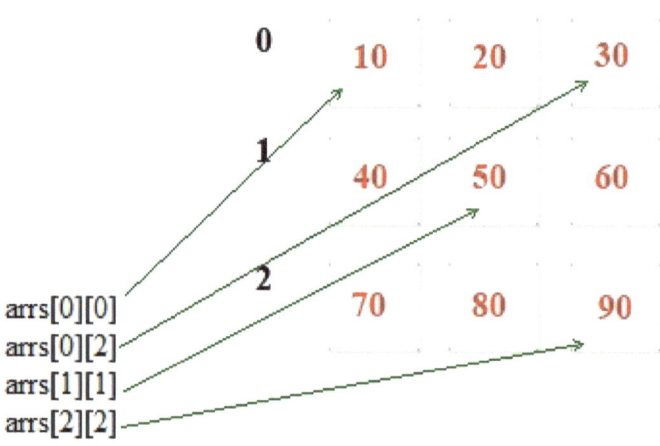

```
using System.Diagnostics;
namespace ConsoleApplication
{
    class BinaryArray
    {
        static void Main(string[] args)
        {
            //Two-dimensional array definition and initialization
            int[,] arrs ={
                        {10,20,30},
                        {40,50,60},
                        {70,80,90}
                    };

            Debug.Write(arrs[0,0] + ",");
            Debug.Write(arrs[0,2] + ",");
            Debug.Write(arrs[1,1] + ",");
            Debug.Write(arrs[2,2]);
        }
    }
}
```

Result:
10,30,50,90

2. Print all data

arrs.Rank: get the number of dimensions of the array.
arrs.GetLength(0): get the number of the array[0].

```csharp
using System.Diagnostics;

namespace ConsoleApplication
{
    class BinaryArray
    {
        static void Main(string[] args)
        {
            int[,] arrs ={
                        {10,20,30},
                        {40,50,60},
                        {70,80,90}
                    };

            // i: row index, j: column index
            for (int i = 0; i <= arrs.Rank; i++)
            {
                for (int j = 0; j < arrs.GetLength(0); j++)
                {
                    Debug.Write(arrs[i,j]+ " ");
                }
                Debug.WriteLine("");
            }
        }
    }
}
```

Result:

10 20 30
40 50 60
70 80 90

Two-Dimensional Array Minesweeper

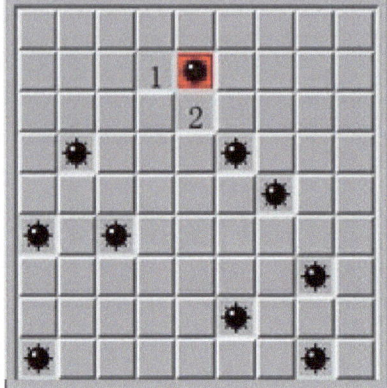

Mine-sweeping game:
 1: no thunder
 2: there is thunder

```csharp
using System.Diagnostics;
using System;
namespace ConsoleApplication
{
    class BinaryArrayMine
    {
        static void Main(string[] args)
        {
            int[,] thundes ={
                        {1,1,1,1},
                        {1,1,1,1},
                        {1,2,1,1},
                        {1,1,1,1}
                    };

            //Keyboard input row number and column number
            Debug.WriteLine("Please enter the row number:");
            int row = Convert.ToInt32(Console.ReadLine());
            Debug.WriteLine("Please enter the column number:");
            int col = Convert.ToInt32(Console.ReadLine());
            int value = thundes[row, col];//value obtained from the array
```

```csharp
            for (int i = 0; i <= thundes.Rank; i++)
            {
                for (int j = 0; j < thundes.GetLength(0); j++)
                {
                    if (value == thundes[i,j] && value == 2)
                    {
                        Debug.Write("Thunder");
                    }
                    else
                    {
                        Debug.Write("* ");
                    }
                }
                Debug.WriteLine("");
            }
        }
    }
}
```

Result:

Please enter the row number:
2
Please enter the column number:
1
* * * *
* * * *
* Thunder* *
* * * *

Struct

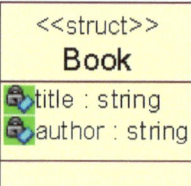

```
using System.Diagnostics;
namespace ConsoleApplication
{
    struct Book
    {
        public string title;
        public string author;
    };

    class Structure
    {
        static void Main(string[] args)
        {
            Book book1;      // declare book1, type is Book

            book1.title = "Easy Learning C#";
            book1.author = "Yang Hu";

            // print Book1 information
            Debug.WriteLine(book1.title);
            Debug.WriteLine(book1.author);
        }
    }
}
```

Result:

Easy Learning C#
Yang Hu

Class

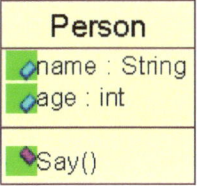

1. Define a Person class
2. There are two attributes in the Person: name, age
3. There is one method in the Person: say()

```csharp
using System.Diagnostics;
namespace ConsoleApplication
{
    class Person
    {
        public string name;
        public int age;

        public void Say()
        {
            Debug.WriteLine("My name is: " + name + ", this year: " + age + " years old");
        }
    }

    class TestEncapsulation
    {
        static void Main(string[] args)
        {
            Person p = new Person();// create a object reference p
            p.name = "Joseph"; //Use the p access attributes and methods
            p.age = 22;
            p.Say();

            Person p2 = new Person();
            p2.name = "David";
            p2.age = 23;
            p2.Say();
        }
    }
}
```

Result:
```
My name is: Joseph, this year: 22 years old
My name is: David, this year: 23 years old
```

Encapsulation Method

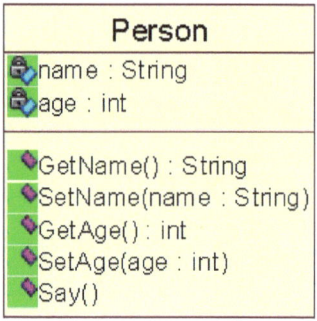

```
using System.Diagnostics;
namespace ConsoleApplication
{
    class Person
    {
        private string name; //private attribute
        private int age;

        //Define a public method to set private attribute
        public void SetName(string name)
        {
            Debug.WriteLine(this); //this: current object
            this.name = name;
        }

        public string GetName()
        {
            return this.name;
        }

        public void SetAge(int age)
        {
            this.age = age;
        }

        public int GetAge()
        {
            return this.age;
        }
```

```csharp
        public void Say()
        {
            Debug.WriteLine("My name is: " + name + ", this year " + age + " years old");
        }
    }

    class TestEncapsulationMethod
    {
        static void Main(string[] args)
        {

            Person p = new Person();
            p.SetName("Joseph");
            p.SetAge(22);
            p.Say();
            Debug.WriteLine(p);
            Debug.WriteLine(p.GetName() + " " + p.GetAge());
        }
    }
}
/**
    1. The variables defined in the class are called member variables.
    2. The variables defined in the method are called local variables
    3. The reference object cannot access the private attribute of the class
    4. If you want to access private attribute, you should provide a public method.
*/
```

Result:

```
ConsoleApplication.Person
My name is: Joseph, this year 22 years old
ConsoleApplication.Person
Joseph 22
```

Constructor Method

Constructor method: is the same method name as class, no return value. When the create a object, the constructor method is called automatically.

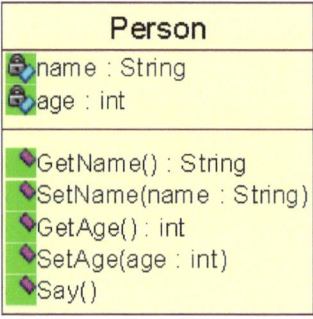

```
using System.Diagnostics;
namespace ConsoleApplication
{
   class Person
   {
      private string name;
      private int age;

      //Define constructor without parameters
      public Person()
      {
         Debug.WriteLine("Person is instantiated");
      }

      //Define the constructor with parameters
      public Person(string name, int age)
      {
         this.name = name;
         this.age = age;
      }

      public void Say()
      {
         Debug.WriteLine("My name is :" + name + ", this year: " + age + " years old");
      }
   }
```

```csharp
class Constructor
{
    static void Main(string[] args)
    {
        Person p = new Person();

        //Instantiate Person with a constructor with parameters
        Person p2 = new Person("Joseph", 22);
        p2.Say();

        //Anonymous object
        new Person("David", 23).Say();
    }
}
```

Result:

```
My name is: Joseph, this year 22 years old
My name is: David, this year 23 years old
```

Method Overload

Method overload: In the same class, there is a method with the same name and different parameter numbers or parameter types.

```
                  Caculator
    Add(a : Integer, b : Integer) : Integer
    Add(a : Double, b : Double) : Double
```

```csharp
using System.Diagnostics;
namespace ConsoleApplication
{
    class Caculator
    {
        public double Add(double a, double b)
        {
            return a + b;
        }

        public int Add(int a, int b)
        {
            return a + b;
        }
    }

    class OverLoad
    {
        static void Main(string[] args)
        {
            Caculator c = new Caculator();
            double result = c.Add(10, 20);
            Debug.WriteLine(result);

            //Call the overload method with different parameter types
            int result2 = c.Add(50, 55);
            Debug.WriteLine(result2);
        }
    }
}
```

Result:
```
30
70.7
```

Static Keyword

static : all objects sharing the same variable and method

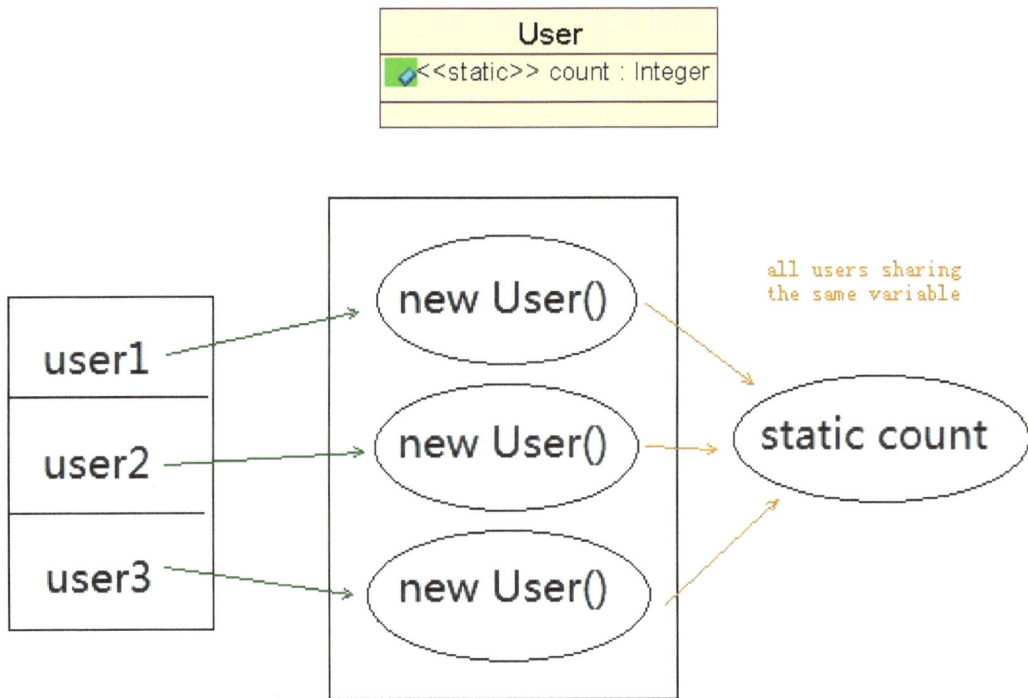

```csharp
using System.Diagnostics;

namespace ConsoleApplication
{
    class User
    {
        public static int count;
    }

    class TestStatic
    {
        static void Main(string[] args)
        {
            User user1 = new User();
            user1.count++;

            User user2 = new User();
            user2.count++;

            User user3 = new User();
            user3.count++;

            Debug.WriteLine("users count: " + User.count);
        }
    }
}
```

Result:

```
users count: 3
```

Inheritance

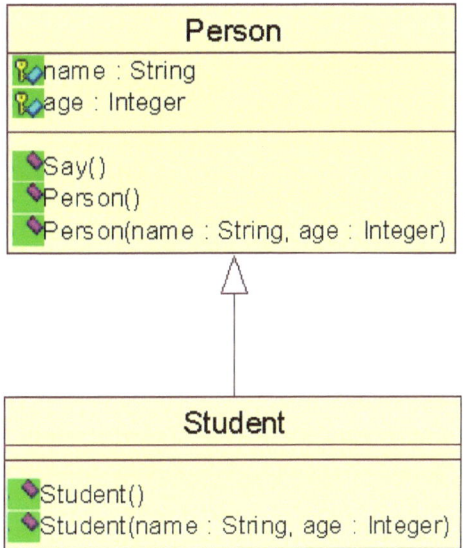

Topic:
Student inherit the Person

Step:
1. Class: Student, Person
2. Relationship: Student extends Person
3. Attributes: Person attributes (name, age)
4. Methods: Person actions (say)

```csharp
using System.Diagnostics;
namespace ConsoleApplication
{
    class Inheritence
    {
        static void Main(string[] args)
        {
            Student s = new Student();
            s.name = "Sumi";
            s.age = 22;
            Student s2 = new Student("Isacc", 23);
            s2.Say();
        }
    }
}
```

```csharp
class Person
{
    public string name;
    public int age;

    public Person()
    {
        Debug.WriteLine("Parent class Person instantiation");
    }

    public void Say()
    {
        Debug.WriteLine("Person can speaking");
    }
}

//Person is called parent class or super class
//Student is called a subclass of Person
class Student : Person
{
    public Student()
    {
        Debug.WriteLine("Subclass Student Instantiation");
    }
    public Student(string name, int age)
    {
        Debug.WriteLine("Subclass Student " + name + " instantiated");
    }
}
/**
    1. The subclass cannot access the private attribute of the parent class
    2. The subclass can access the protected, public attribute of the parent class.
*/
```

Result:
```
parent class Person instantiation
Subclass Student Instantiation
the parent class of  Person instantiated
Subclass Student Isacc instantiated
Person can speaking
```

Method Override

Override: the subclass overwrites the method of the parent class, the instance of the subclass will call the method of subclass, not call the method of the parent class.

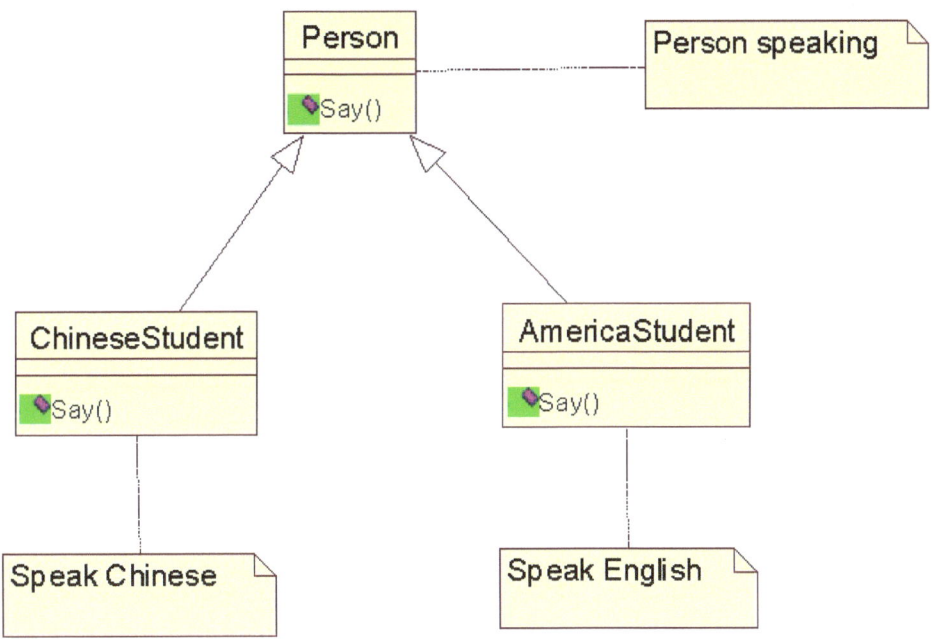

```
using System.Diagnostics;
namespace ConsoleApplication
{
    class Override
    {
        static void Main(string[] args)
        {
            ChineseStudent chineseStudent = new ChineseStudent();
            chineseStudent.Say();

            AmericaStudent americaStudent = new AmericaStudent();
            americaStudent.Say();
        }
    }
}
```

```csharp
class Person
{
    public void Say()
    {
        Debug.WriteLine("Person speaking");
    }
}

class ChineseStudent : Person
{
    public void Say()
    {
        Debug.WriteLine("Speak Chinese");
    }
}

class AmericaStudent : Person
{
    public void Say()
    {
        Debug.WriteLine("Speak English");
    }
}
```

Result:

```
Speak Chinese
Speak English
```

Abstract Class

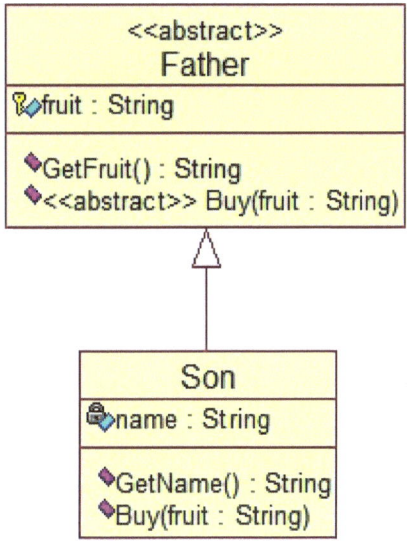

Topic:
Dad told me to buy a pound of fruit

Step:
1. Abstract class: Father
2. Relationship: Son inherits Dad
3. Method: Buy (buy) the father called his son to buy fruit, but father not buy

```csharp
using System.Diagnostics;

namespace ConsoleApplication
{
    class TestAbstract
    {
        static void Main(string[] args)
        {
            Son s = new Son("Luke");

            s.Buy("Fruit");

            Debug.WriteLine("Dad, Dad, I bought a pound: " + s.GetFruit());
        }
    }
}
```

```csharp
abstract class Father
{
    protected string fruit;

    public string GetFruit()
    {
        return this.fruit;
    }

    //Declare that you want to buy fruit
    public abstract void Buy(string fruit);
}

class Son : Father
{
    private string name;
    public Son(string name)
    {
        this.name = name;
    }

    //The son fulfills the requirement of his father to buy fruit
    public override void Buy(string fruit)
    {
        this.fruit = fruit;
    }

    public string GetName()
    {
        return this.name;
    }
}
/**
    1. The abstract method can't have a method body implementation, only the method declaration
    2. If a subclass inherits an abstract class, the subclass must implement all the abstract methods of the parent class.
    3. Abstract classes cannot be instantiated directly, they must be instantiated by subclasses
*/
```

Result:
```
Dad, Dad, I bought a pound: Fruit
```

Interface

interface: Interface is a convention

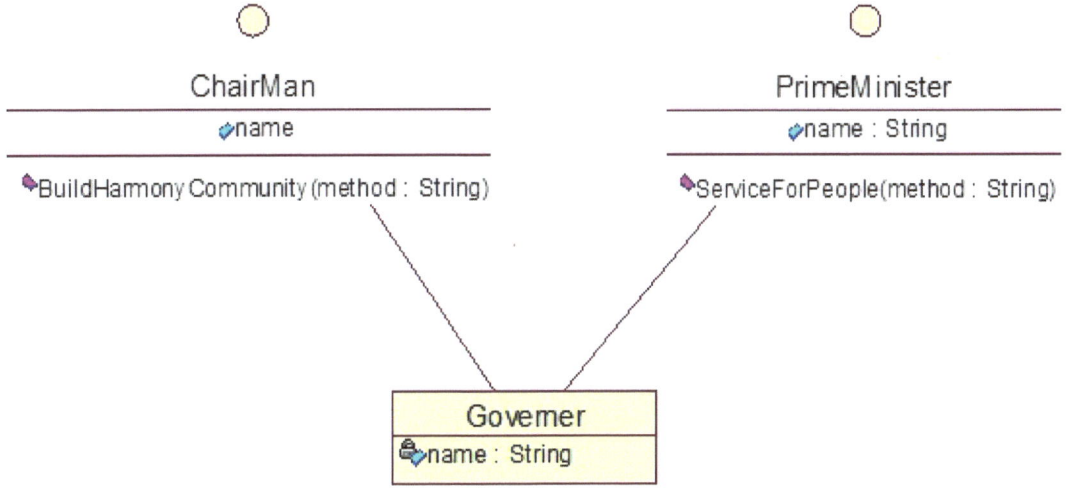

Topic: Chairman says to Establish a Harmonious Society

```csharp
using System.Diagnostics;
namespace ConsoleApplication
{
    interface ChairMan
    {
        string name = "ChairMan";
        void BuildHarmonyCommunity(string method);
    }

    class Governer : ChairMan
    {
        private string name;
        public Governer(string name)
        {
            this.name = name;
        }

        public void BuildHarmonyCommunity(string method)
        {
            Debug.WriteLine(name + " build harmony community by " + method);
        }
```

```
        public string getName()
        {
            return this.name;
        }
    }

    class TestInterface
    {
        static void Main(string[] args)
        {
            Debug.WriteLine(ChairMan.name);

            Debug.WriteLine("Start conferences...");
            Governer g1=new Governer("Governer");
        }
    }
}
/**
    1. The implementation of the method is not allowed in the interface.
    2. The subclass must implement all the declaration methods in the interface.*/
```

Result:

```
ChairMan
Start conferences...
Governer build harmony community by Education
```

Enum

Topic:
　　Draw a variety of different circles on the drawing board

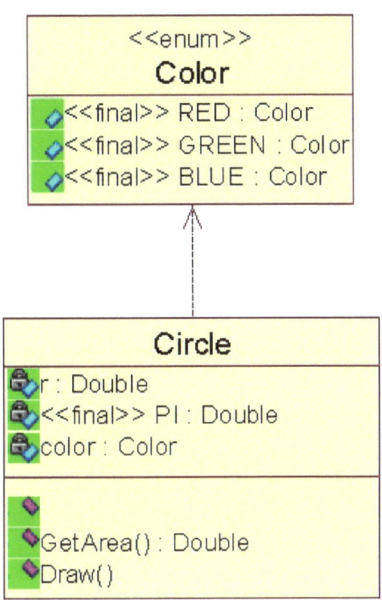

```csharp
using System.Diagnostics;
namespace ConsoleApplication
{
    enum Color
    {
        RED, GREEN, BLUE
    }

    class Circle
    {
        double r;//Radius of the circle
        const double PI = 3.14;
        Color color;//Round color (0: red 1: green 2: blue)

        public Circle(double r, Color color)
        {
            this.r = r;
            this.color = color;
        }

        public double GetArea()
        {
            return PI * r * r;
        }

        public void Draw()
        {
            string colorName = "";
            if (color == Color.RED)
            {
                colorName = "Red";
            }
            if (color == Color.GREEN)
            {
                colorName = "Green";
            }
            if (color == Color.BLUE)
            {
                colorName = "Blue";
            }
            Debug.WriteLine("draw circle  area: " + GetArea() + " color: " + colorName);
        }
    }
}
```

```csharp
class TestEnum
{
    static void Main(string[] args)
    {
        // r=5
        Circle red = new Circle(5, Color.RED);
        //red.PI=1000;
        red.Draw();

        // r=10
        Circle green = new Circle(10, Color.GREEN);
        green.Draw();

        // r=20
        Circle blue = new Circle(20, Color.BLUE);
        blue.Draw();
    }
}
```

Result:

```
draw circle  area: 78.5 color: Red
draw circle  area: 314.0 color: Green
draw circle  area: 1256.0 color: Blue
```

Polymorphism

Polymorphism: method overload, method override, object up and down transformation
Subclass objects can be converted to parent objects.

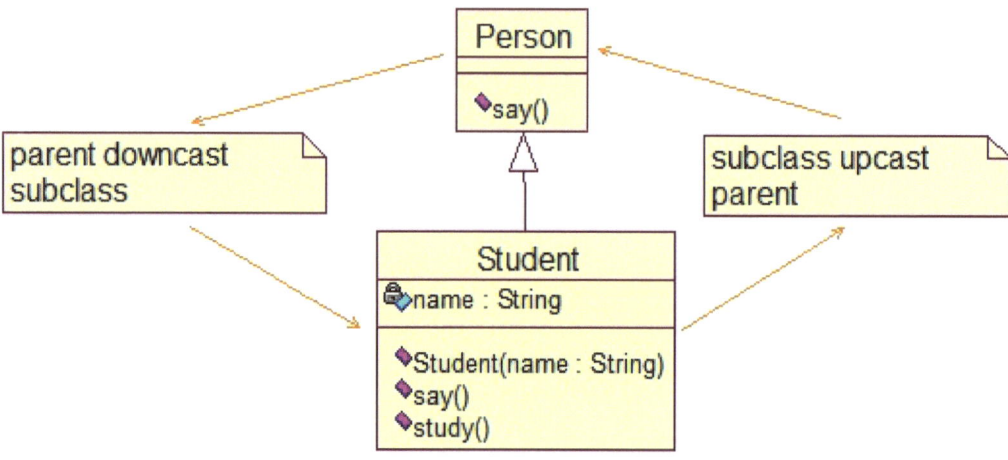

```csharp
using System.Diagnostics;
using System;
namespace ConsoleApplication1
{
    class Person
    {
        public void Say()
        {
            Debug.WriteLine("Person speaking");
        }
    }

    class Student : Person
    {
        private String name;

        public Student(String name) {
            this.name = name;
        }

        public void Say() {
            Debug.WriteLine("Student speak english");
        }
```

```csharp
        public void Study() {
            Debug.WriteLine("study");
        }
    }

    public  class Polymorphism5
    {
        public static void Main(String[] args) {

            //Upcast.
            Person p = new Student("David");
            p.Say();

            //Downcast
            Student s = (Student)p;
            s.Say();
            s.Study();
        }
    }
}
```

Result:

```
Student speak english
Student speak english
Study
```

Polymorphism

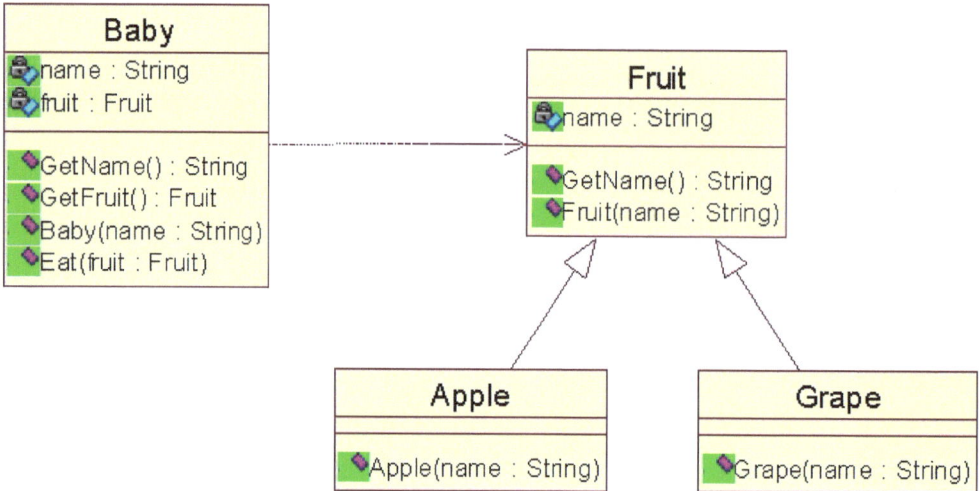

Topic:
    Children Eat Fruits (Apples, Grapes)
Step:
    1. Class: Baby, Fruit (Apple, Grape)
    2. Relationship: Fruit -> Child (apple, grape)
    3. Attributes: Baby (name, fruit)
    4. Methods: eat(Fruit fruit)

```csharp
using System.Diagnostics;
namespace ConsoleApplication
{
   class Baby
   {
      protected Fruit fruit;
      protected string name;

      public string GetName()
      {
         return this.name;
      }

      public Fruit GetFruit()
      {
         return this.fruit;
      }
```

```csharp
        public override void Eat(Fruit fruit)
        {
            this.fruit = fruit;
        }
    }

    class Fruit
    {
        protected string name;

        public string GetName()
        {
            return this.name;
        }
    }


    class Grape : Fruit
    {
        public Grape(string name)
        {
            this.name = name;
        }
    }


    class Apple : Fruit
    {
        public Apple(string name)
        {
            this.name = name;
        }
    }
```

```csharp
class Polymorphism5
{
    static void Main(string[] args)
    {
        Baby baby = new Baby("Gajia");

        Apple apple = new Apple("Red apple");
        Grape grape = new Grape("Black grape");

        p.Eat(apple);
        Debug.WriteLine(baby.GetName() + " eat " + baby.getFruit().GetName());
        p.Eat(grape);
        Debug.WriteLine(baby.GetName() + " eat " + baby.getFruit().GetName());
    }
}
```

Result:

```
Gajia eat Red apple
Gajia eat Black grape
```

Thread

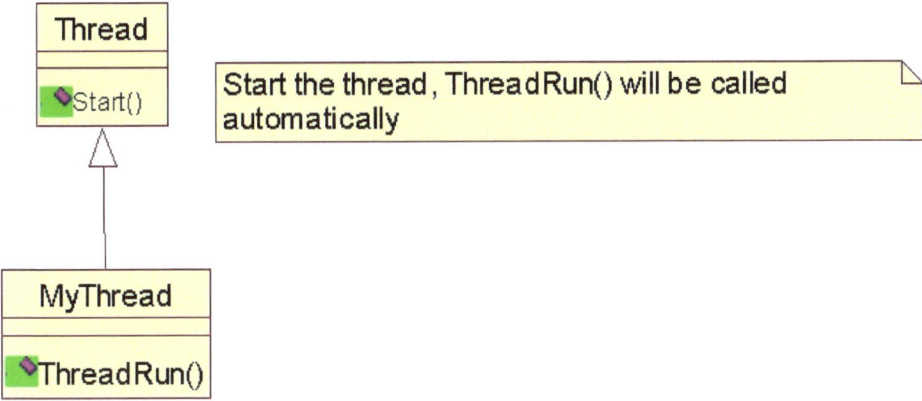

1. If you want to start a thread you must call start() method
2. The thread runs at the same time, the CPU allocates to each thread for a period of time to execute.

```csharp
using System.Diagnostics;
using System.Threading;
namespace ConsoleApplication
{
    class TestThread
    {
        static void Main(string[] args)
        {
            MyThread mythread = new MyThread();

            //Start the thread, ThreadRun()) will be called automatically
            Thread thread = new Thread(new ThreadStart(mythread.ThreadRun));
            thread.Start();

            for (int i = 0; i < 10; i++)
            {
                Debug.WriteLine("Main Thread " + i);
                Thread.Sleep(1000); //Sleep 1 second = 1000 millisecond
            }
        }
    }
}
```

```csharp
class MyThread
{
    public void ThreadRun()
    {
        for (int i = 0; i < 10; i++)
        {
            Debug.WriteLine("MyThread " + i);
            Thread.Sleep(1000);
        }
    }
}
```

Result:

```
Main Thread 0
Main Thread 1
Main Thread 2
MyThread 0
Main Thread 3
MyThread 1
Main Thread 4
Main Thread 5
Main Thread 6
Main Thread 7
MyThread 2
Main Thread 8
Main Thread 9
MyThread 3
MyThread 4
MyThread 5
MyThread 6
MyThread 7
MyThread 8
MyThread 9
```

Exception

try {

Running exception ← → Running normally

} catch (Exception e) {

} finally {

}

```
using System.Diagnostics;
using System;

namespace ConsoleApplication
{
    class TestException
    {
        static void Main(string[] args)
        {
            Caculator c = new Caculator();
            c.div(10, 0); // Running exception
            Debug.WriteLine("div finished execution");
        }
    }
}
```

```csharp
class Caculator
{
    public int div(int a, int b)
    {
        int result = 0;        try
        {
            // When the exception jump to the catch to execute
            result = a / b;
            Debug.WriteLine("Normal execution");
            return result;
        }
        catch (Exception e)
        {
            Debug.WriteLine("Divisor cannot be 0");
        }
        finally
        {
            Debug.WriteLine("finally the last free release");
        }
        Debug.WriteLine("Result return");
        return 0;
    }
}
```

Result:

```
Normal execution
finally the last free release
div finished execution
```

String Functions

1. String comparison
    1. == : Reference comparison
    2. equals: Value comparison

```csharp
using System.Diagnostics;
namespace ConsoleApplication1
{
    class TeststringEquals
    {
        static void Main(string[] args)
        {
            string str1 = "Dreams";
            string str2 = "Dreams";
            Debug.WriteLine(str1 == str2);
            Debug.WriteLine(str1.Equals(str2));

            Debug.WriteLine("----------------------------------------");

            string str3 = "hello";
            string str4 = "Hello";
            Debug.WriteLine(str3.Equals(str4));

            string str = "Children's Songs";
            Debug.WriteLine(str.StartsWith("Children"));

            string fileName = "c:/media/gequ.mp3";
            Debug.WriteLine(fileName.EndsWith(".mp3"));
        }
    }
}
```

Result:

```
True
True
----------------------------------------
False
True
True
```

2. String replacement

```csharp
using System.Diagnostics;
namespace ConsoleApplication1
{
    class TeststringEquals
    {
        static void Main(string[] args)
        {
            string article = "our motherland is the grassland";
            Debug.WriteLine(article);

            article = article.Replace("grassland", "garden");
            Debug.WriteLine(article);
        }
    }
}
```

Result:

```
our motherland is the grassland
our motherland is the garden
```

3. Substring

```csharp
using System.Diagnostics;
namespace ConsoleApplication1
{
    class TeststringEquals
    {
        static void Main(string[] args)
        {
            string filePath = "e:\\book\\music.mp3";

            //Cut the extension of the file
            string fileExtension = filePath.Substring(filePath.IndexOf('.'));
            Debug.WriteLine(fileExtension);

            //Cut the name of the file
            fileName = filePath.Substring(filePath.LastIndexOf('\\') + 1);
            Debug.WriteLine(fileName);
        }
    }
}
```

Result:

```
.mp3
music.mp3
```

4. String Split

```csharp
using System.Diagnostics;
namespace ConsoleApplication1
{
    class TeststringEquals
    {
        static void Main(string[] args)
        {
            //enter the language, math, and physics of a student
            string scores = "100;98;95";
            //Split the scores by ;
            string[] scoreArray = scores.Split(new char[1] { ';' });

            Debug.WriteLine("language=" + scoreArray[0]);
            Debug.WriteLine("math=" + scoreArray[1]);
            Debug.WriteLine("physics=" + scoreArray[2]);
        }
    }
}
```

Result:

```
language=100
math=98
physics=95
```

String And StringBuilder

String is *immutable*, meaning String cannot be changed once created. To solve this problem, C# introduced StringBuilder. StringBuilder is a *dynamic object* that allows you to expand the number of characters in the string. It doesn't create a new object in the memory but dynamically expands memory to accommodate the modified string.

```csharp
using System.Diagnostics;
using System;
using System.Text;

namespace ConsoleApplication1
{
    class TestStringBuilder
    {
        static void Main(string[] args)
        {
            StringBuilder sb = new StringBuilder();
            for (int i = 0; i < 10; i++)
            {
                str += i + ",";
                sb.Append(i).Append(",");
            }
        }
    }
}
```

Result:

0,1,2,3,4,5,6,7,8,9,

Date

```csharp
using System.Diagnostics;
using System;

namespace ConsoleApplication1
{
    class TestDate
    {
        static void Main(string[] args)
        {
            DateTime dt = DateTime.Now;

            Debug.WriteLine(dt.ToString());
            Debug.WriteLine(dt.Year.ToString());
            Debug.WriteLine(dt.DayOfWeek.ToString());
            Debug.WriteLine(dt.DayOfYear.ToString());
            Debug.WriteLine(dt.Month.ToString());
            Debug.WriteLine(dt.Hour.ToString());
            Debug.WriteLine(dt.Minute.ToString());
            Debug.WriteLine(dt.Second.ToString());
            Debug.WriteLine(dt.Millisecond.ToString());

            // Calculate the difference in days between 2 dates
            DateTime dt1 = Convert.ToDateTime("10-1-2018");
            DateTime dt2 = Convert.ToDateTime("10-15-2018");
            TimeSpan span = dt2.Subtract(dt1);
            int dayDiff = span.Days + 1;
            Debug.WriteLine(dayDiff);

            // Add one day to the date, reduce one day
            Debug.WriteLine(dt.AddDays(1)); //Add one day
            Debug.WriteLine(dt.AddDays(-1));//Reduce one day

        }
    }
}
```

Result:

```
2019/4/5 8:23:13
2019
Friday
95
4
8
23
13
430
15
2019/4/6 8:23:13
2019/4/4 8:23:13
```

Generic

Generic : can pass various data types

```csharp
using System.Diagnostics;
namespace ConsoleApplication1
{
    class Person<T>
    {
        private T age;

        public Person(T age)
        {
            this.age = age;
        }

        public T GetAge()
        {
            return age;
        }
    }

    class TestGeneric
    {
        static void Main(string[] args)
        {
            Person<string> p = new Person<string>("30");
            Debug.WriteLine(p.GetAge().GetType());

            Person<int> p2 = new Person<int>(28);
            Debug.WriteLine(p2.GetAge().GetType());
        }
    }
}
```

Result:

```
System.String
System.Int32
```

List

ArrayList:
1. ArrayList in order of first-in, first-out.
2 ArrayList is an array of objects

0	1	2	3
Advanced King Room	Twin Room	Family Room	Business Room

```csharp
using System.Diagnostics;
using System.Collections;
using System.Collections.Generic;
namespace ConsoleApplication1
{
    class Room
    {
        private string roomName;
        private double price;

        public Room(string roomName, double price)
        {
            this.roomName = roomName;
            this.price = price;
        }

        public string RoomName
        {
            get
            {
                return roomName;
            }
            set
            {
                this.roomName = value;
            }
        }
```

```csharp
        public double Price
        {
            get
            {
                return price;
            }
            set
            {
                this.price = value;
            }
        }
    }

    class TestHotel
    {
        static void Main(string[] args)
        {
            List<Room> roomList = new List<Room>();

            roomList.Add(new Room("Advanced King Room", 290));
            roomList.Add(new Room("Twin Room", 290));
            roomList.Add(new Room("Family Room", 332));
            roomList.Add(new Room("Business Room", 332));

            Debug.WriteLine("Hotel Room Information");
            foreach (Room room in roomList)
            {
                Debug.WriteLine(room.RoomName + "," + room.Price);
            }
        }
    }
}
```

Result:

```
Hotel Room Information
Advanced King Room,290
Twin Room,290
Family Room,332
Business Room,332
```

Queue

Queue: first-in first-out object collection

Topic:
Print the car information that according to the order.

```csharp
using System.Diagnostics;
using System.Collections;
using System.Collections.Generic;
namespace ConsoleApplication1
{
    class TestQueue
    {
        static void Main(string[] args)
        {
            Queue<Car> station = new Queue<Car>();

            // Add into the queue
            station.Enqueue(new Car("Mercedes", 100));
            station.Enqueue(new Car("BMW", 200));
            station.Enqueue(new Car("Honda", 300));

            Car car = station.Dequeue(); // Out queue
            Debug.WriteLine(car.getName() + "," + car.getVolume());

            car = station.Dequeue(); // Out queue
            Debug.WriteLine(car.getName() + "," + car.getVolume());

            car = station.Dequeue(); // Out queue
            Debug.WriteLine(car.getName() + "," + car.getVolume());

        }
    }
}
```

```
class Car
{
   private string name;
   private double volume;

   public Car(string name, double volume)
   {
      this.name = name;
      this.volume = volume;
   }

   public string getName()
   {
      return name;
   }

   public void setName(string name)
   {
      this.name = name;
   }

   public double getVolume()
   {
      return volume;
   }

   public void setVolume(double volume)
   {
      this.volume = volume;
   }
}
```

Result:

```
Mercedes,100
BMW,200
Honda,300
```

Stack

Stack: first-in last-out object collection

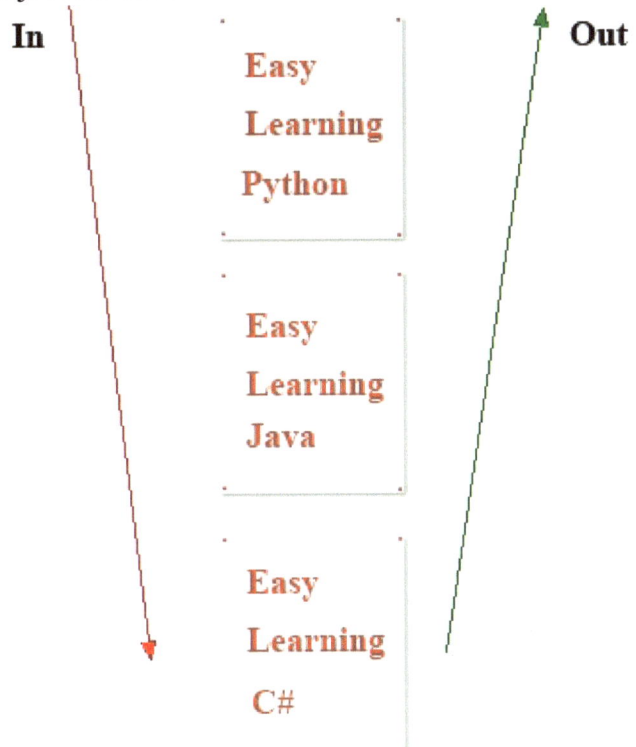

Topic:
box can put a lot of books, Print all book

```csharp
using System.Diagnostics;
using System.Collections;
using System.Collections.Generic;
namespace ConsoleApplication1
{
    class TestStack
    {
        static void Main(string[] args)
        {
            Stack stack = new Stack();
            // Push book
            stack.Push("Easy Learning C#");
            stack.Push("Easy Learning Java");
            stack.Push("Easy Learning Python");

            // Pop book
            string book = stack.Pop().ToString();
            Debug.WriteLine(book);

            book = stack.Pop().ToString();
            Debug.WriteLine(book);

            book = stack.Pop().ToString();
            Debug.WriteLine(book);
        }
    }
}
```

Result:

```
Easy Learning Python
Easy Learning Java
Easy Learning C#
```

Hashtable

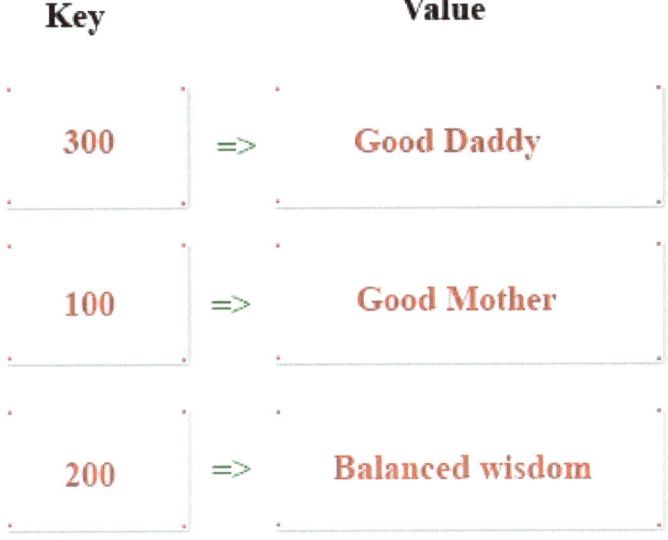

```
using System.Diagnostics;
using System.Collections;
using System.Collections.Generic;

namespace ConsoleApplication1
{
    class TestHashtable
    {
        static void Main(string[] args)
        {
            Hashtable hashtable = new Hashtable();
            hashtable.Add("300", "Good Daddy");
            hashtable.Add("100", "Good Monther");
            hashtable.Add("200", "Balanced wisdom");

            Debug.WriteLine(hashtable["100"]);// get the value according to the key
            ICollection key = hashtable.Keys; // Get the collection of keys
            foreach (string k in key)
            {
                Debug.WriteLine(k + " : " + hashtable[k]);
            }
        }
    }
}
```

Result:

```
100 : Good Monther
200 : Balanced wisdom
300 : Good Daddy
```

File

```csharp
using System.Diagnostics;
using System;
using System.IO;

namespace ConsoleApplication
{
    class TestFile
    {
        static void Main(string[] args)
        {
            FileInfo f = new FileInfo(@"C:\Users\tim\Desktop\test.txt");

            //Get the file last modified date
            Debug.WriteLine(f.LastWriteTime.ToString());

            //Get the file last access time
            Debug.WriteLine(f.LastAccessTime.ToString());

            //Get the file creation time
            Debug.WriteLine(f.CreationTime.ToString());

            // Get the file size
            Debug.WriteLine(f.Length.ToString());

            //Get file attribute
            Debug.WriteLine(f.Attributes);

            //file path
            Debug.WriteLine(f.DirectoryName);

            //Append file
            StreamWriter sw = File.AppendText(@"C:\Users\tim\Desktop\test.txt");
            sw.WriteLine("benchmarking life");
            sw.WriteLine("Keep going");
            sw.WriteLine("Forrest Gump");
            sw.Flush();
            sw.Close();
```

```csharp
            //Copy the file
            string orignFile;
            string newFile;
            orignFile = @"C:\Users\tim\Desktop\test.txt";
            newFile = @"C:\Users\tim\Desktop\copy.txt";
            File.Copy(orignFile, newFile, true);

            //Delete Files
            string delFile = @"C:\Users\tim\Desktop\copy.txt";
            File.Delete(delFile);

            // Move files
            orignFile = @"C:\Users\tim\Desktop\test.txt";
            newFile = @"C:\Users\tim\Desktop\testmove.txt";
            File.Move(orignFile, newFile);

        }
    }
}
```

Directory

```csharp
using System.Diagnostics;
using System.Collections;
using System.Collections.Generic;
using System;
using System.IO;
namespace ConsoleApplication
{
    class TestDirectory
    {
        static void Main(string[] args)
        {
            FindFile(@"E:\Email");
        }

        static void FindFile(string sourcePath)
        {
            //Find files in the directory and subdirectories, list subdirectories and files
            DirectoryInfo dir = new DirectoryInfo(sourcePath);
            DirectoryInfo[] dirSub = dir.GetDirectories(); // Get subdirectories
            if (dirSub.Length <= 0)
            {
                foreach (FileInfo f in dir.GetFiles("*.*", SearchOption.TopDirectoryOnly))
                {
                    Debug.WriteLine(dir + @"\" + f.ToString());
                }
            }

            foreach (DirectoryInfo d in dirSub)//find subdirectories
            {
                FindFile(dir + @"\" + d.ToString());
                Debug.WriteLine(dir + @"\" + d.ToString());

                foreach (FileInfo f in dir.GetFiles("*.*", SearchOption.TopDirectoryOnly))
                {
                    Debug.WriteLine(dir + @"\" + f.ToString());
                }
            }
        }
    }
}
```

Thanks for learning
https://www.amazon.com/dp/B08F39C488

If you enjoyed this book and found some benefit in reading this, I'd like to hear from you and hope that you could take some time to post a review on Amazon. Your feedback and support will help us to greatly improve in future and make this book even better.

You can follow this link now.

http://www.amazon.com/review/create-review?&asin=109278800X

Different country reviews only need to modify the amazon domain name in the link:
www.amazon.co.uk
www.amazon.de
www.amazon.fr
www.amazon.es
www.amazon.it
www.amazon.ca
www.amazon.nl
www.amazon.in
www.amazon.co.jp
www.amazon.com.br
www.amazon.com.mx
www.amazon.com.au

I wish you all the best in your future success!

www.ingramcontent.com/pod-product-compliance
Lightning Source LLC
Chambersburg PA
CBHW041314180526
45172CB00004B/1092